CONTENTS

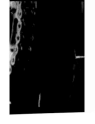

ABOUT MOTORCYCLES

A motorcycle is a two-wheeled vehicle that is powered by an engine. It can serve as an economic means of travel or can be used for sporting purposes.

Motorcycles

The first gasoline-powered motorcycle was invented in 1885, when Gottlieb Daimler and Wilhelm Maybach attached an engine to a modified bicycle. As early as 1867, however, two American inventors demonstrated a 2-wheeled vehicle powered by steam propulsion. The first motorcycle available to buy went on the market in 1894 and the rest, as they say, is history!

Motorcycle designs are becoming ever more hi-tech.

Their Popularity

Generally speaking, people choose bikes because they are an economic and convenient means of transport. They usually cost less than a car, use less fuel, are quicker through traffic and are easier to park. Motorcycles, these days, are extremely popular. Around the world, various motorcycle clubs have formed. These clubs go for road trips and enjoy various activities together on their bikes.

Many Types

There are many different types of motorcycle: touring bikes are heavy and suitable for long distance travel, being designed to carry heavy luggage; sports bikes are lightweight and fast, usually with aerodynamic bodywork; off-road bikes come with big suspension forks and shock absorbers and usually have large rugged tires for grip; cruisers are bulky motorcyles with a riding position that places the feet forward and the hands raised, tilting the rider back slightly for a more comfortable ride over long distances.

Did You Know?

The first motorcycle available for purchase was the Hildebrand & Wolfmüller (1894). Only a few hundred were ever made.

Cruisers are recognized for their long and low design.

DUCATI 1098R

The Ducati 1098R is the ultimate super bike. The lightest, most technologically advanced, and most powerful two-cylinder motorcycle ever built. The R stands for race bike.

Road-legal Race Bike

Ducati claim that the 1098R is as close to the race bike as they have ever produced. It generates 180 horsepower and weighs 165 kg (364 lbs). The 0-60 mph time is less than 2.5 seconds and top speed is 186 mph. The bike has distinctive design features such as a high tail section, compact front end, along with a non-integrated exhaust system. Superior components and advanced electronics deliver a high level of performance.

The Supertest World Association (SWA) awarded the 1098R the "*Best Bike of the Year*" in 2008.

Did You Know?

The Ducati 1098R has the highest torque-to-weight ratio of any sports bike.

The Engine

The aim of the engine designers was to create an ultra-compact engine that was more efficient and more powerful than previous engines for the next generation of Ducati super bikes. To keep the engine light but still strong, the designers used titanium, magnesium alloy and carbon fiber. The engine produces an amazing 180 horsepower. The engine has a unique 'W' shape, created by its twin-cylinder formation. A six gear transmission allows the bike to take full advantage of the speed produced.

The Testastretta Evoluzione engine on the 1098R is the lightest Ducati super bike engine ever.

The Body

The 1098R has the soul of a race bike. The riding position is such that man and machine become one. The basic frame weighs just 9 kg (19.8 lbs). The bike has a highly **aerodynamic** shape. The bike is fitted with an array of electronic equipment to enhance bike control.

TECHNICAL INFO

Class: Sport
Engine: V-Twin
Power: 180 hp
@ 9,750 rpm
(revolutions per minute)

The 1098R carries trademark Ducati features like the high tail section, compact front-end and twin under-seat silencers.

DUCATI SUPERBIKE 749

The Ducati Superbike 749 is the perfect super bike entry model and ideal for riders looking to experience their first thrill of riding a high-performance machine.

The Bike

The Ducati Superbike 749 incorporates many features from the 999 model. The L-twin Testastretta engine is very compact, making the finished motorcycle narrow and agile, much like its racing cousin. The 748 cc Testastretta engine supplies 108 hp. It has a smaller rear tire, an adjustable rake and five-position adjustable rearset mounts.

A digital display occupies center place on the dashboard of the 749.

Ducati reduced the size of the 749's rear tire to improve performance.

TECHNICAL INFO
Class: Superbike
Engine: L-twin
Power: 107 hp @ 10,000 rpm
Weight: 188 kgs (414 lbs)

The Features

The 749 is powered by a Ducati Testastretta engine. The bike has features that are the result of decades of research and development. These include advanced electronics, state-of-the-art **ergonomics** and the best aerodynamics in its class. The front suspension guarantees better stability and, consequently, better bike control.

 At the heart of the 749 is the powerful Testastretta engine.

The 749 is perfect for people who are riding a superbike for the first time.

The Look

The Ducati 749's tubular trellis frame is designed for the racetrack. The suspension, both front and rear, is adjustable, resulting in a smooth ride. The Ducati 749 has two versions: regular and the new 749 Dark. The 749 Dark is the more accessible of the two, perhaps because of its darker and more stylish look. The 749 is a perfect model for the first-time rider who wants to experience the thrill of riding a Ducati.

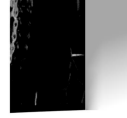

DUCATI 999S

The Ducati 999S is a combination of power, style and comfort. It is designed for riders of all sizes and is a user-friendly performance bike.

The Race Bike

The Ducati 999S is an exciting sports bike. Long and narrow with a sleek look, the 999S showcases Ducati's experience gained over years of success at the highest levels of racing. Designed by Pierre Terblanche, it is known as an extremely high-performance, race-ready motorcycle. The 999S is at the top of its class thanks to its engine performance and outstanding weight distribution.

TECHNICAL INFO
Class: Sport
Engine: L-twin
Power: 143 hp
@ 9,750 rpm
Weight: 186 kgs
(410 lbs)

The 749's outstanding weight distribution made for one of the best-handling motorcycles ever seen.

The Testastretta

The 999S features an especially powerful **Testastretta** engine that delivers 143 hp. This engine has been tried and tested on the racetrack, and is designed to give maximum output even when the the bike is accelerating or cornering. The engine has been designed with the most experienced riders in mind, who expect the best in terms of technology and performance. All in all the Testastretta engine offers the bike higher power, better performance, and greater reliability.

 The 999S's engine is built to the highest levels of performance.

Other Features

The motorcycle has an adjustable riding position that provides the rider comfort and control on the road as well as the racetrack: the position of the footpegs, rake, **suspension**, plus seat/tank combination on the single-seat version, are all modifiable. The bulky front end ensures precise control and is designed to reduce pressure on the rider's wrists. A wider steering angle makes the motorcycle easy to ride in the streets.

The 999S can be set up for optimum ride quality on road or track.

HONDA CBR125R

Though relatively smaller in size, the CBR125R has the look and the feel of a sports bike. It comes at a much cheaper price compared to bigger models, and is a popular entry-level model for bike lovers the world over.

Small and Convenient

The CBR125R has pared down sports bike proportions and a four-stroke **powerplant** that gives it respectable power for its 125 cc engine. Though not designed for the race tracks, it looks like a **racing** motorcycle. In the UK, the bike is especially popular among younger riders who do not yet have the license to ride more powerful machines.

The Honda CBR125R is a fun and accessible entry-level sports bike.

Did You Know?

The Honda CBR125R was the best-selling bike in the UK in 2005.

The Performance

Powered by a liquid-cooled, 4-stroke engine, the CBR125R gives reasonable performance for its size, and for a first-time biker it's a dream. The subsequent smooth **acceleration** makes this motorcycle fun and exciting to ride. The fuel-injection system delivers the right amount of fuel for best performance. The CBR125R also gives off lower **emissions** and has better fuel economy than previous models.

The Look

The racing bike-inspired seat blends smoothly into the tank, making for a comfortable ride. The forward-leaning riding position mimics more powerful sports bikes, with the rider straddling the fuel tank and controlling the bike into corners with precision.

The Honda CBR125R stands out with its aggressive, slim sports bike styling.

TECHNICAL INFO
Class: Sport
Engine: Single Cylinder
Power: 13 hp
Weight: 115 kgs
(254 lbs)

HONDA CBR1000RR

The Honda CBR1000RR is a bike designed to burn up the racetrack! On its release in 2004, the bike was noted for a number of new technological elements unseen on a motorcycle before.

```
TECHNICAL INFO
Class: Sport
Engine: In-line four
Power: 178 hp
@ 12,000 rpm
Weight: 176 kgs
        (388 lbs)
```

Racing-Meets-Super Bike

The Honda CBR1000RR merges racing technology into a super bike and is an excellent ride on the track as well as the streets. With a comparatively lighter engine and chassis compared to other similarly-sized motorcycles, it is able to deliver more power to the wheels and makes for extreme performance.

The Honda CBR1000RR is designed to perform on the racetrack.

The Powerplant

Perhaps the best feature of this motorcycle is the liquid-cooled 998 cc four-stroke engine. The engine was designed specifically with an eye toward handling as well as **horsepower**. Special attention was given to ensuring the powerplant remained an extremely compact package. This compact engine was then positioned further forward on the bike's **chassis** for an improved weight distribution.

Enviable Features

The Honda CBR1000RR comes with a high-capacity 350-watt AC generator. The LED taillights and folding aerodynamic mirrors embellish the appearance. There is a plastic tank shell cover that protects the airbox and the tank. A one-piece fan assembly efficiently cools the engine and there is an ignition switch/**fork** lock for greater security. To improve the handling, Honda engineers also lightened as many pieces as possible.

The four cylinder engine is the most outstanding feature of the CBR1000RR.

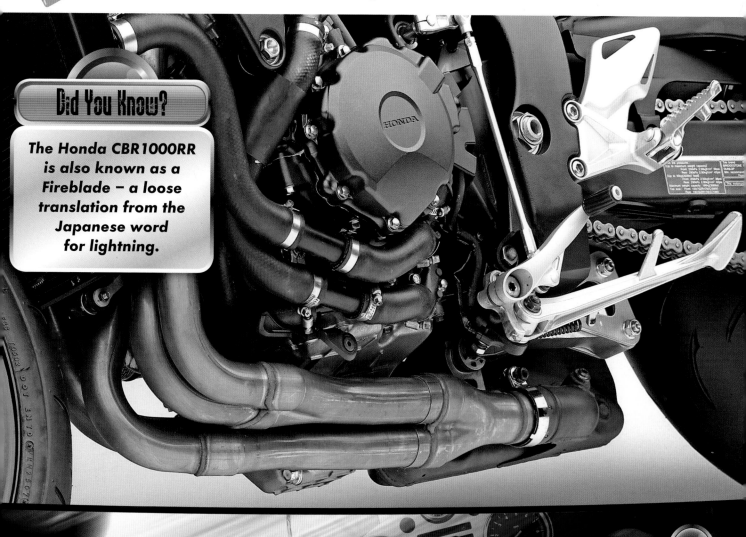

Did You Know?

The Honda CBR1000RR is also known as a Fireblade – a loose translation from the Japanese word for lightning.

HONDA SHADOW SPIRIT 750 C2

The Honda Shadow Spirit 750 C2 is one of Honda's finest cruising motorcycles. Easy to manoeuvre, this motorcycle is a combination of power and style.

Long and low, the Shadow Spirit is a landmark Honda bike.

Long and Low

The Shadow Spirit 750 C2 is a long motorcycle, with a low-slung seat similar to larger-engined heavyweight cruisers. The user-friendly ergonomics and handling comfort makes it a good motorcycle for first-time riders. The single backbone frame of the motorcycle gives it a longer wheelbase, and the stretched shape accommodates physically larger riders. Fortunately, the seat is only 65 cm (25.7 inches) from the ground, so most riders find the bike accommodating.

TECHNICAL INFO

Class: Cruiser
Engine: In-line four
Power: 131 bhp
@ 14,000 rpm
Weight: 228 kg
(503 lbs)

Oodles of Attitude

Every element of the Shadow Spirit's design shrieks out attitude. The new handlebar offers a sporty, upright riding position. The low scooped-out seat and a teardrop-shaped air cleaner cover add to the hot-rod aura. Other signature elements of the Shadow Spirit include the rear fender, with a custom, integrated taillight, a chromed, tank-mounted instrument panel and twin, bullet-style mufflers.

 The Shadow Spirit offers the perfect seating position: low and upright.

Easy Handling

Despite its weight (228 kg (503 lbs)), the Honda Spirit 750 C2 is relatively easy to **manoeuvre** for a bike of its size. Similarly, the larger and narrower front wheel makes for light and agile handling when cruising over distance.

 With its easy manoeuverability, the bike has become a very popular cruiser.

KAWASAKI NINJA ZX-6R

The middleweight Kawasaki Ninja ZX-6R is a sleek machine, with the soul of a bigger bike. Manufactured with high-end technology, it is known for being easy to ride.

A *High-performance Bike*

The Ninja ZX-6R offers the high performance of a big motorcycle combined with the handling characteristics of a smaller machine. In keeping with Kawasaki's racing philosophy, the ZX-6R is considered an ideal motorcycle for the middleweight sports bike category.

 The Kawasaki Ninja ZX-6R is a middleweight sports bike, first introduced in 1995.

Low Friction

The Ninja ZX-6R's powerplant was specially designed to minimize friction. The low-friction powerplant makes the motorcycle more responsive, and easier to guide into corners with only minor adjustments. The components are strong and more compact, resulting in a much smaller engine. This has allowed the chassis designers to create a slim and compact chassis.

Easy Handling

One of the best features of the Kawasaki Ninja ZX-6R is its ease of handling, with the bike responding instantly and precisely to the rider's every command. A compact, lightweight design allows it to maintain speed through the turn. The entire package of frame, suspension, engine and bodywork is designed to offer a more exciting ride.

The ZX-6R impresses on the race track.

Did You Know?

The Kawasaki Ninja ZX-6R was the first middleweight sports bike with an aluminum frame.

KAWASAKI NINJA ZX-10R

Technology

The Kawasaki Ninja ZX-10R was designed for the racetrack. It has an advanced chassis technology and greater horsepower than other open-class supersport motorcycles. It seems that the engineers have also kept in mind the street riders while designing this motorcycle, demonstrated by the stability and the ease of handling.

The Ninja ZX-10R is a high-performance sports bike, hailed as the best super bike in the world upon its release.

The Kawasaki Ninja ZX-10R is designed for the racetrack but can be ridden on the streets as well.

Did You Know?

The Kawasaki Ninja ZX-10R is capable of going from 0-60 mph in just 2.9 seconds.

Highlights

This racing monster is powered by a 998 cc high-performance engine. The wheels feature a new six spoke design that are as light as racing wheels. Street riders will appreciate the bike's solid stability and predictable handling. The Kawasaki Ninja ZX-10R has an efficient **exhaust** system that not only flows better than the ZX-9R but gives off less noise and emissions as well.

Power all the Way

The ZX-10R is designed for the racing enthusiast. The bike is built for the accomplished rider who can fully appreciate its capabilities. Whether put to the test at a racetrack, or merely the focus of racing conversation, the bike is, by all standards, the embodiment of the ultimate super bike.

TECHNICAL INFO
Class: Sport
Engine: In-line four
Weight: 175 kgs
(386 lbs)

The ZX-10R has a very efficient exhaust system that keeps noise and emissions to a minimum.

KAWASAKI VULCAN 900 CUSTOM

The Kawasaki Vulcan 900 Custom has great looks, is powerful, and comes with features that are uniquely different from other bikes.

Looks

The Kawasaki Vulcan 900 Custom has the power and feel of a bigger motorcycle. It is designed to stand out from the rest. The sleek bodywork, the big rear tire and the slender-looking front end makes this motorcycle a true eye catcher.

Features

Kawasaki's engineers have delivered a motorcycle that provides the customized appearance you'd expect from an expensive, exclusive motorcycle. The combination of the low rear end and the slender front end is perfect. But it is not just pretty looking. The V-Twin engine gives it the necessary **torque** and power.

 The Kawasaki Vulcan 900 Custom has everything: great looks and great power.

The Custom Bike

The Vulcan 900 Custom's contrasting front and rear end is completemented by the teardrop-shaped fuel tank. The sculpted bodywork of the bike add to the custom feel, which is topped off by the slim, oversized, 21 inch front wheel, with specially designed spokes.

The Kawasaki Vulcan 900 Custom is a mean machine for a mid-sized cruiser.

Did You Know?

The Kawasaki Vulcan 900 Custom comes in three colours: Metallic Diablo Black, Passion Red and Candy Lime Green.

TECHNICAL INFO
Class: Custom Cruiser
Engine: 903 cc, V-twin, 4-stroke
Weight: 249 kgs (549 lbs)

KAWASAKI VULCAN 900 CLASSIC

The Vulcan 900 is a medium sized motorcyle designed for cruising purposes. Possibly the most powerful in its class, this motorcycle is a very similar cousin of the Kawasaki Vulcan 900 Custom.

The Look

The 900 Classic is a mid-size cruiser with the look and feel of a bigger motorcycle. With well-defined lines and an uncluttered look, the Vulcan 900 Classic is the ideal bike for the cruiser lover. It is relatively easy to handle for first-time riders and those wanting a heavyweight motorcycle feel on a mid-size package.

The Powerplant

The 900 Classic's 903 cc engine offers excellent acceleration. The curved engine fins give a flashier look to the traditional big, fuel-injected V-twin powerplant. The bike has perhaps the best torque and power ratios in the mid-size cruiser class. Add to that its spacious seating and the motorcycle becomes the ideal cruiser.

Other Features

The designers have complemented the engine of the 900 Classic with added ergonomics. The chrome-accented air cleaner and headlight are typical of cruiser stylings. Other features include an LED taillight, sleek bodywork and a low seat that gives the smaller rider necessary comfort. The freshly-styled fenders and fuel tank add beautiful curves to the traditional cruiser shape.

Did You Know?

The 900 Classic had the biggest engine of any mid-weight cruiser until Yamaha introduced the V-Star 950 in September 2008.

The 900 Classic may be a mid-size cruiser but it has the feel of a larger bike.

BMW K1200LT

The BMW K1200LT is a large touring bike. It is easy to handle and engineered for comfort over long stretches of road.

Touring in Style

The BMW K1200LT is a touring motorcycle with many excellent features. A high-output powerplant, an advanced gearbox, chrome package, and an electro-hydraulic center stand, make this motorcycle among the most comfortable imaginable. An advanced damper system on the suspension helps smooth out the bumps and keep the bike stable over long distances.

Did You Know?

The BMW K1200LT even has lights that illuminate the ground for mounting and dismounting the bike at night!

The BMW K1200LT is designed for long distance touring.

Cruising Along

The K1200LT is powered by a water-cooled 1,173 cc engine that generates about 100 horsepower. The bike comes with a 60 ampere alternator that puts out 840 watts of electrical power – so you can run a lot of electrical gadgets while on the road. The bike handles well both on long-distance touring and all-round riding. The six-speed gearbox allows the rider easy acceleration or deceleration, and an overall smooth ride.

A Bike With Everything

The K1200LT has an on-board computer that tells you the temperature, average speed, and fuel consumption. The bike's console features a vast array of lights, buttons and indicators. There is ample storage space for luggage, an on-board entertainment system and even heated handle grips and seats for those cold days!

Perhaps the best feature of the K1200LT is its on-board computer.

BMW CRUISER R 1200 C MONTAUK

The BMW Cruiser R 1200 C Montauk is the latest evolution of BMW's unique cruiser class. This bike has been manufactured with cutting-edge design and is smooth and comfortable to ride, as well as being extremely reliable.

The Cruiser

The Montauk is not a super bike; at least not in the racing sense. The motorcycle is at its best when it is in cruise mode at average revs. It is more tough-looking than other cruisers, which was the objective of the engineers when they got down to designing this cruiser. All in all, it one of BMW's most stylish bikes, with good power and reliable drivetrain and brakes.

The Montauk is a tough-looking cruiser.

Everything You Need...

The 1,170 cc powerplant generates 61 horsepower. The Montauk gets its own wide handlebar, Telelever fork, front fender, small windshield and unique stacked dual headlights with a larger beam over a smaller one. The seat is more sculpted with a small passenger pad. The bike comes with heated grips, a tachometer, and a clock.

... With Excellent Handling

The Montauk rides much smoother than some other BMW cruisers. The riding position is comfortable and the short windshield offers some wind protection. The front wheel is bulky, but the wide handlebar and the reduced weight of the cruiser allow the motorcycle to turn well, even under breaking.

Did You Know?

The BMW R 1200 C Montauk has even featured in a James Bond movie.

BMW K1200S

The BMW K1200S is a super bike in the truest sense of the word. Contemporary looking, it is a powerful machine as well.

The Technology

The BMW K1200S is an engineering masterpiece, with a combination of high-end technology, design and performance. The motorcycle can accelerate from 0-60 mph in less than 3 seconds. The K1200S is performance personified.

The K1200S is contemporary in design and powerful as well.

The Powerplant

The compact, liquid-cooled, four-cylinder powerplant is set across the frame instead of along. The engine bank, the main part of the engine, is angled forwards at 55 degrees, improving the steering and front wheel traction – a prerequisite for a powerful motorcycle like the BMW K1200S. But its most outstanding feature is its full electronic controls for dampers and springs.

A Thrilling Ride

The chassis of the BMW K1200S reacts well under all conditions, with good response and feedback from the front wheel. A radical suspension, innovative technologies and advanced brakes make this bike a thrilling ride.

The rear of the bike contains a small storage space.

```
TECHNICAL INFO
Class: Sport
Engine: In-line four
Power: 167 hp
@ 10,250 rpm
Weight: 227 kg
      (500 lbs)
```

BMW R1200R

The compact BMW R1200R is a powerful machine. Do not be fooled by its sleek looks; this is a versatile and genuine all-rounder.

A Bike with Attitude

The BMW R1200R is all about attitude. A motorcycle capable of exhilarating performance, the R1200R has the horsepower and acceleration to satisfy the adrenaline junkie. It has the latest version of BMW's Integral Anti-lock Braking System and an Automatic Stability Control System. The motorcycle is indeed exciting.

Every aspect of the R1200R has attitude.

Sleek and Light

The R1200R's 1,170 cc engine generates 109 hp, with an oil-cooler fitted behind the wheel fork. The rear section of the motorcycle's frame has been specially constructed, giving the motorcycle a sleek appearance and reducing its overall weight.

Did You Know?

The BMW R1200R's average fuel consumption is 50 miles per gallon.

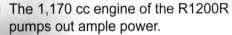 The 1,170 cc engine of the R1200R pumps out ample power.

Understated Body

The compact-looking R1200R has noticeably understated body components. This is purposefully done to highlight the technical features of the machine, and of the engine in particular. The headlight is contemporary, with free-form reflectors integrated in to the rest of the motorcycle's body, creating a tough-looking front end.

BMW R1150RS

The BMW R1150RS is a touring motorcycle with most of the attributes a rider looks for: reliability, decent speed and comfort.

Not for Racing

The BMW R1150RS is not designed for speed, but rather is designed for comfort, stability and smooth riding over long distances. Though not as glamorous as the other motorcycles in the BMW cruiser class, this tourer is highly user-friendly.

Did You Know?

RT stands for Reise-Tourer, or Travel Tourer. BMW launched their first RT in the late 1970's.

The BMW R1150RS is designed for long journeys.

Long Distance Runner

The four-valve, 1,130 cc twin engine features six-speed transmission. The big screen provides protection from wind and harsh weather. The throttle is smooth and responsive. This tourer is not the fastest on two wheels, but with a top speed of 134 mph, it gives the rider enough to get excited about.

A Comfortable Ride

The riding position is comfortable. The handle bars even come with heated grips for use in cold weather! The screen and handlebars are adjustable, as is the wide and well-padded seat, which is important on such a big, heavy bike weighing 246 kgs (542 lbs).

TECHNICAL INFO
Class: Touring
Engine: Two-cylinder boxer
Power: 95 hp @ 7,500 rpm
Weight: 246 kg (542 lbs)

The big boxer engine of the R1150RS provides lots of acceleration.

BIG DOG K-9

This dog is truly big! At 2.7 meters (9 feet) long, it can be a bit of a handful for some riders. The pared down design is a combination of tough and sleek. One thing's for sure: the K-9 is a motorcycle that will turn heads!

Did You Know?

The Big Dog K-9 has a 300mm- (11.8 inch-) wide rear tire!

The Really Big Dog

The K-9 is one of the best chopper models to come from Big Dog, a famous name in custom motorcycles. It is a really BIG bike, with a length of 2.7 meters (9 feet). For a bike of its size, the K-9 offers surprising ease of handling and control, and awesome power.

The Big Dog K-9 stands out from the crowd.

Monster Features

The K-9 weighs close to 330 kgs (728 lbs) and, as with most custom bikes from the Big Dog stable, has a distinctively fat rear tire. the 39 degree front rake (angle from the handlebars to the front wheel) combines with the narrow tank to exaggerate the length.

Other features include billet wheels, a 2-into-1 exhaust, and two-piece rotors. The braking is delivered by the four-piston billet calipers.

Monster Looks

This monster bike also comes with an A-frame swingarm suspension that makes riding over long distances and rough terrain a surprisingly comfortable experience. All in all, the K-9 looks the part of a custom bike – cool and heavily styled, with stripped-back bodywork and oversized front forks.

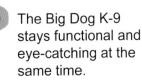

TECHNICAL INFO
Class: Chopper
Engine: V-twin
Weight: 328 kgs
(723 lbs)

The Big Dog K-9 stays functional and eye-catching at the same time.

MTT TURBINE

This is the most powerful bike in the world! It's also one of the longest and, not to mention, most visually striking!

Turbine Engine

The MTT Turbine is only the world's second wheel driven motorcycle powered by a turbine engine. The engine is mounted upside down on a custom aluminum frame. The MTT is powered by a converted Rolls Royce Allison 250 series turboshaft engine that is capable of producing up to 320 hp!

Beauty Meets Technology

The body is made of lightweight carbon fiber panels. There are two slash-cut exhausts that disperse the heat. The motorcycle also represents the latest in cutting-edge technology, featuring carbon fiber fairings, rear mounted camera equipped with an LCD colour display, a radar detector with laser scrambler, a one touch "Smart Start" ignition, and much more.

 The MTT Turbine is driven by a turbine engine that has been converted and re-built.

These converted turbine engines start life on aircraft such as helicopters.

The Beast

The motorcycle has a reported top speed of 227 mph and comes with a hefty price tag — a cool $150,000US! Indeed, when it was launched it was recognized by Guinness World Records as the most powerful and most expensive production motorcycle in the world. Riding this machine is believed to be quite a handful due to the sudden acceleration and its long body.

FACTS AND RECORDS

Sylvester Roper built the first self-propelled two-wheeled machine in America. Roper's steam-powered bicycle made its first public appearance in 1869 in his hometown of Roxbury, Massachusetts.

The first gasoline-powered motorcycle was developed by Gottlieb Daimler in 1885.

When motorcycles were first produced they were very popular with women. In fact in 1915, Avis and Effie Hotchkiss, rode from New York to San Franciso. They took a circuitous route covering over 5,000 miles.

Another early motorcycle heroine was Bessie Stringfield, a.k.a. the Motorcycle Queen of Miami. She made eight solo-cross country trips and was a motorcycle dispatch rider. The fact that Bessie was not only a woman, but also African-American, were enormous obstacles of the time to her achievement. At first, she couldn't even get a motorcycle license in Miami, Florida. However, a police officer interceded on her behalf.

The most popular motorcycle company before World War I was the Indian Motorcycle Company. After the war, Harley Davidson took over the number one spot until 1928, when DKW became the leading motorcycle manufacturer in the world.

On September 5, 2006, Chris Carr of Stockton, California, broke the motorcycle land speed world record at the Bonneville Salt Flats (Utah). His fastest run was measured at 354 mph (567.8 km/h).

The Dodge Tomahawk from Chrysler is the world's fastest concept bike. It is powered by a 500 horsepower engine, has four wheels and is potentially capable of 400 mph!

The world's most expensive bike is the Ecosse titanium series, priced at a whopping $275,000.

The Fire Bike was a custom chopper, created by the custom bike company Orange County Choppers, as a tribute to the firefighters who died in the terrorist attacks of 9/11.

.

The Indian motorcycle manufacturer, Hero Honda, is the world's largest manufacturer of two wheelers.
Its Hero Honda Splendor model is the highest selling motorcycle in automotive history, having sold more then 8.5 million units.

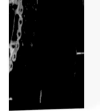

GLOSSARY

Acceleration: The increase in the rate of speed of something

Aerodynamic: A shape that helps reduce the drag caused by air moving past it

Cc: Cubic centimetre: a metric unit of measurement used in relation to the size of a vehicle's engine

Chassis: The frame of a motorcyle or other vehicle, to which other components are attached

Components: Parts

Cruiser: Motorcycle meant for cruising purposes

Displacement: The quantity of fuel held by a fuel tank

Emissions: Gasses that are produced by the combustion engine and released through the exhaust

Ergonomic: Something that is designed for ease of use and comfort through its design

Exhaust: The parts of an engine that discharge waste gasses

Horsepower (hp): A measurement of power

Integrated: Something that is built in

Manoeuvre: To control direction or movement of something

Powerplant: The engine of a motorcycle

Suspension: A system of springs and shock absorbers that connects the bike to its wheels

Testastretta: Engine used in Ducati bikes

Torque: The effect of force that causes an object to rotate in relation to the transfer of engine power to the wheels

Tourer: Motorcycle meant for touring purposes

INDEX